SING, CHOIRS!

Anthems, psalms and hymns for choirs

Edited by John Baird

T0061452

SING, CHOIRS!

Anthems, psalms and hymns for choirs

Edited by John Baird

NOVELLO

Published by
Novello Publishing Limited
14-15 Berners Street,
London W1T 3LJ, UK.

Exclusive Distributors:
Music Sales Limited
Distribution Centre, Newmarket Road,
Bury St Edmunds, Suffolk IP33 3YB, UK.

Music Sales Pty Limited
Units 3-4, 17 Willfox Street, Condell Park
NSW 2200, Australia.

Order No. NOV294382
ISBN 978-1-78305-414-5

Music processed by Paul Ewers Music Design.
Project Manager: Jonathan Wikeley.

Printed in the EU.

www.musicsalesclassical.com

CONTENTS

MASS MOVEMENTS

HYMNS AND HYMN-ANTHEMS

PSALM SETTINGS

ANTHEMS

★Pieces with asterisks all arr. John Baird.

INTRODUCTION

Sing, Choirs! is a library in miniature. It contains many of the Christian church's popular, traditional anthems, including at least one example that will be suitable for each of the major services of the year.

A number of Anglican chants (Psalms, Magnificat and Nunc dimittis) is included, set out in a way that should enable those who are unfamiliar with the style to perform them easily. The selection of movements from the Mass can be used to enrich the music of the liturgy in services.

Many of the works are presented in their original form, such as Bruckner's *Locus iste*, Mozart's *Laudate Dominum* and Byrd's *Ave verum corpus*. Others are arrangements, adaptations or longer pieces, abridged to bring them into the scope of a useable anthem, including choral arrangements of Handel's *Largo* and *Ave Marias* by Schubert and Bach/Gounod. This collection has practicability as a priority. The keyboard parts can be played on either the piano or the organ.

Much of the music will be suitable for special occasions making *Sing, Choirs!* an indispensable volume for choirs singing weekly church services, weddings and funerals, and in the concert hall.

John Baird
Wandsworth Common, February 2014

Palestrina: **Kyrie** (p. 4)

Each of the three sections can provide a separate piece, particularly suitable for introits.

Haydn: **Hosannas & Benedictus** (p. 22)

Using the intonation allows this to be a fully fledged Sanctus for liturgical purposes. If not singing the Benedictus, then omit the small B♭ in bar 16.

Howells: **All my hope on God is founded** (p. 31)

At last, an opportunity to sing Howells's great tune in harmony.

Gibbons: **Come, Holy Ghost** (p. 32)

Finishing your performance by repeating bars 1–12 gives a pleasant ABA structure.

Parry: **Dear Lord and Father of mankind** (p. 33)

As with the Howells hymn, this provides the opportunity to sing this great melody from Parry's oratorio, *Judith*, in four parts.

Nicolai/Bach/Cornelius: **How brightly shines the Morning Star** (p. 34)

Bach doesn't usually repeat the last phrase in his harmonisations but I think it makes for a more rounded piece of music if you do. Cornelius's harmonisation is an arrangement of the chorale as used in his song *Die Könige* from his Christmas Songs op. 8. The song can combine with this harmonisation. You can feel free to add Cornelius's melody in the familiar way.

Beethoven: **Ode to Joy** (p. 38)

The word 'Elysium' is pronounced 'Eloosium'.

Bach: **O sacred head, sore wounded** (p. 40)

The iconic text, 'O sacred head, sore wounded', starts both of these settings from Bach's *St Matthew* Passion.

Wagner: **Praise God, from whom all blessings flow** (p. 46)

For maximum effect the organist should play a B♭7 chord over which the choir sings its opening unison.

Baird: **Alleluia** (p. 59)

Do not attempt to sing this too quickly! The 'descant' in bars 14 – 15 should be sung if forces allow – especially the second time through. The antiphons can be used when appropriate.

Bach/Gounod: **Ave Maria** (p. 71)

The Prelude in C, from Bach's *Well Tempered Clavier*, seems to have acquired an extra bar (27) in the late 18th century – which Gounod includes in this setting.

Byrd: **Ave verum corpus** (p. 83)

If needed, cuts can be made from bar 7 ('Virgine') or bar 14 ('homine') to bar 44 (fourth beat).

Gaudete (p. 108)

If you choose sometimes to sing two refrains between verses, then it is very effective when the last bar of the first refrain is sung as a half bar. An improvised tambourine accompaniment can be very successful.

Handel: **Glory to God** (p. 110)

This chorus will feel more rounded when the recitatives which introduce it in *Messiah* are sung.

Adam: **O holy night!** (p. 152)

As Adam ends both these verses with '*Noël. Noël…le Rédempteur*', I have, similarly, repeated the words 'O holy night' at the same point.

Purcell: **Thou knowest, Lord, the secrets of our hearts** (p. 174)

Either or both of the pair of crotchets in bars 2 can be replaced by a minim.

For Penny, Medici Choir and the singers of
St. Mary Magdalene Church at Wandsworth Common.

Kyrie eleison

(St. Anthony Chorale)

attrib. Franz Josef Haydn (1732-1809)
arr. John Baird

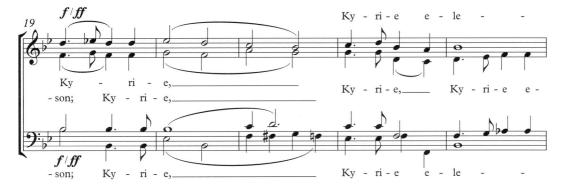

Kyrie eleison

(Missa brevis)

Giovanni Pierluigi da Palestrina
(1525-94)

Gloria in excelsis

(Gloria)

Antonio Vivaldi (1678-1741)

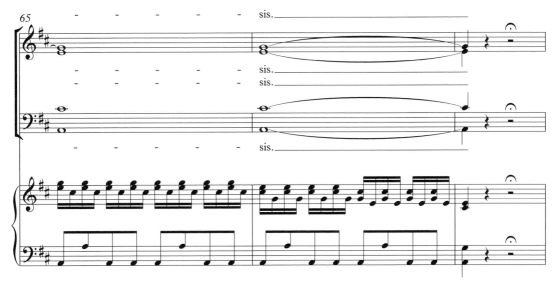

Glo - ri - a in ex - cel - sis De - o.

Sanctus

(Requiem)

Gabriel Fauré (1845-1924)

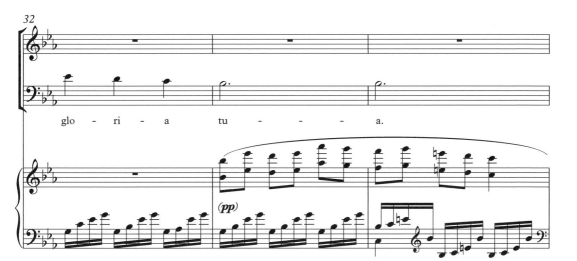

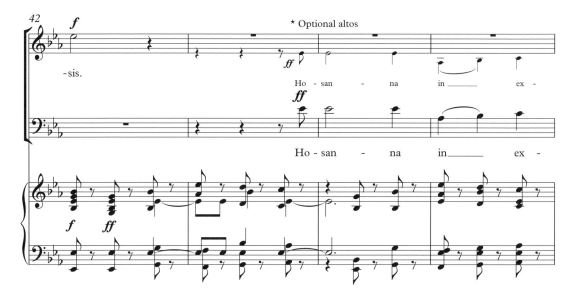

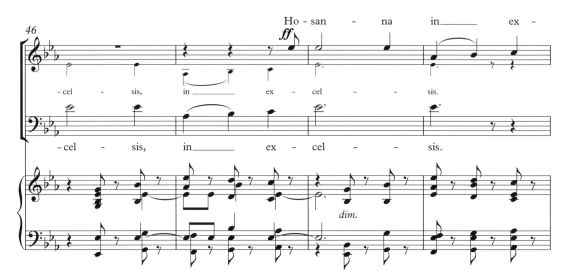

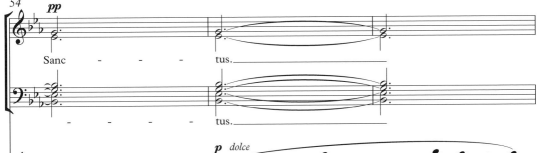

Hosannas & Benedictus

(Missa in tempore belli)

Franz Joseph Haydn (1732-1809)
abridged John Baird

* Optional intonation if singing as part of a mass setting.

1st time only

26

for Valerie, Ruth and David

Agnus Dei

John Baird

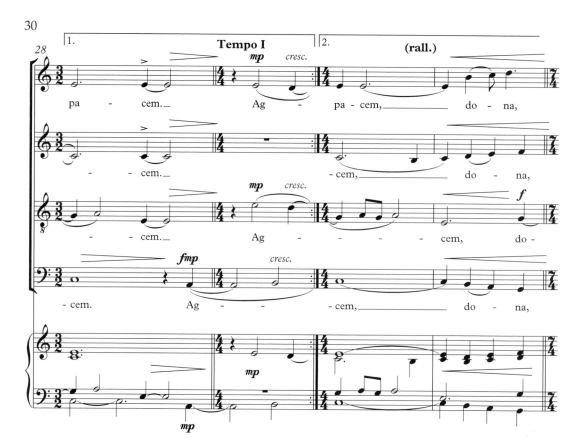

Dedicated to H.H. on his 120th anniversary

All my hope on God is founded

Robert Bridges (1844-1930)
after August Neander (1789-1850)

Herbert Howells (1892-1983)
adapted for SATB by John Baird

*small notes for organ or optional divisi.

for Flora and Natalie

Come, Holy Ghost

George Wither (1588-1667) (Song 44) Orlando Gibbons (1583-1625)
adapt. John Baird

for Benedickt and Fabian

Dear Lord and Father of mankind

John Whittier (1807-92)

C.H.H. Parry (1848-1918)
arr. John Baird

2. In simple trust like theirs who heard,
Beside the Syrian sea,
The gracious calling of the Lord,
Let us, like them, without a word
Rise up and follow thee.

3. O Sabbath rest by Galilee!
O calm of hills above,
Where Jesus knelt to share with thee
The silence of eternity,
Interpreted by love!

4. Drop thy still dews of quietness
Till all our strivings cease;
Take from our souls the strain and stress,
And let our ordered lives confess
The beauty of thy peace.

5. Breathe through the heats of our desire
Thy coolness and thy balm;
Let sense be dumb, let flesh retire;
Speak through the earthquake, wind, and fire,
O still small voice of calm!

34

How brightly shines the Morning Star!

Philipp Nicolai
tr. Rev. H.N. Bate

Melody: Philipp Nicolai (1566-1608)
harm. J.S.Bach (1685-1750)

I

May accompany the solo part in
Cornelius's The Kings *(Die Könige)*

harm. Peter Cornelius (1824-74)
arr. for SATB by John Baird

for the friends in St Mary Magdalene

Drop, drop, slow tears

(Song 46)

Phineas Fletcher (1582-1650)

Orlando Gibbons (1583-1625)
adapt. John Baird

1. Drop, drop, slow tears, and bathe those beau-teous feet, Which brought from heav'n the news and Prince of peace.

2. Cease not, wet eyes, his mer-cies to en-treat; To cry for ven-geance sin doth nev-er cease.

3. In your deep floods drown all my faults and fears; Nor let his eye see sin, but through my tears.

* All three verses may be sung to the music of bars 1 to 7.

Let the people praise the Lord

H.F. Lyte (1793-1847)
adapt. John Baird

Richard Wagner (1813-83)
from *The Mastersingers of Nuremberg* (Act I)
adapt. John Baird

for Anita and Peter, David and Ali

Ode to Joy

Friedrich Schiller (1759-1805)   (Symphony No. 9)   Ludwig van Beethoven (1770-1827)
English words: Timothy Rees (1874-1939)   arr. John Baird
& *The Foundling Hospital Collection*

* Schiller's original words may be sung in addition to, or as an alternative to the English words.

O sacred head, sore wounded

Paul Gerhardt (1607-76)
from a 14th-century Latin hymn
tr. Robert Bridges (1844-1930)

harm. J.S. Bach (1685-1750)
(from *St Matthew Passion*)

I

O sac-red head, sore wound-ed, De-filed and put to scorn; O king-ly head, sur-round-ed With mock-ing crown of thorn; What sor-row mars thy gran-deur? Can death thy bloom de-flower? O coun-ten-ance whose splen-dour The hosts of heav'n a-dore.

II

O sac - red head,_ sore wound - ed, De - filed and_ put to_ scorn; O_

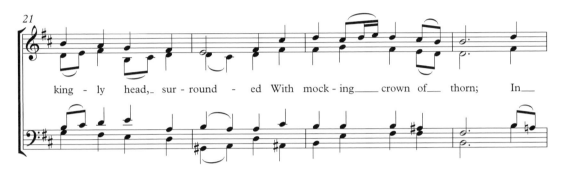

king - ly head,_ sur - round - ed With mock - ing_ crown of_ thorn; In_

this_ thy bit - ter pas - sion My_ heart_ to_ share_ doth_ cry,_ With

thee_ for_ my_ sal - va - tion Up - on the cross_ to_ die._

for Rory

Silent night

Joseph Mohr (1792-1848)
tr. John Freeman Young
(1820-85) & others

Franz Grüber (1787-1863)
arr. John Baird

Sleepers wake!

Philipp Nicolai from Matthew 25
tr. Catherine Winkworth (1827-78)
adapt. John Baird

Philipp Nicolai (1566-1608)
harm. J.S. Bach (1685-1750)

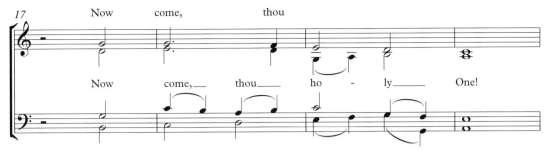

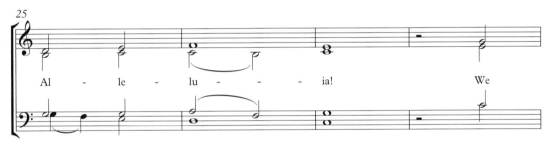

for Caroline and Peter

Praise God, from whom all blessings flow

Thomas Ken (1637-1711)
& William Kethe (d. 1594)

Richard Wagner (1813-83)
from *The Mastersingers of Nuremberg* (Act III)
adapt. John Baird

Magnificat

Luke 1: 46-55

John Goss (1800-80)
after Martin Luther (1483-1546)

1. My soul doth magnify the Lord: And my spirit hath re-joiced in God my Saviour.

2. For he hath re - garded: The lowli - ness of his handmaiden.

3. For be - hold from henceforth: All gene - rations shall call me blessed.

4. For he that is mighty hath magni - fied me: And ho - ly is his name.

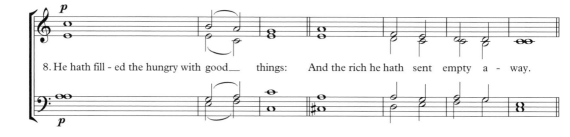

49

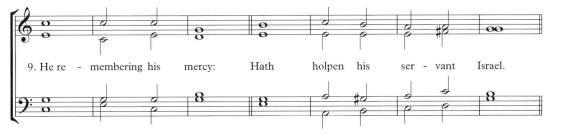

9. He re - membering his mercy: Hath holpen his ser - vant Israel.

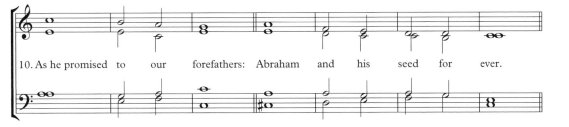

10. As he promised to our forefathers: Abraham and his seed for ever.

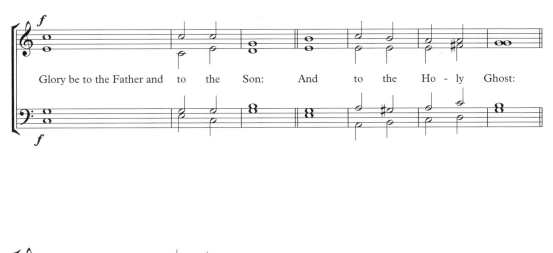

Glory be to the Father and to the Son: And to the Ho - ly Ghost:

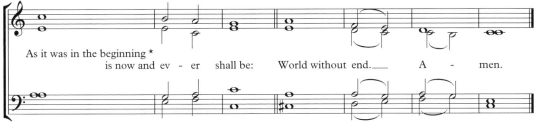

As it was in the beginning *
is now and ev - er shall be: World without end.___ A - men.

for Connor

Psalm 23

Dominus pascit me

Percy Woodstone (1804-82) after
Ludwig van Beethoven (1770-1827)
adapt. & arr. John Baird

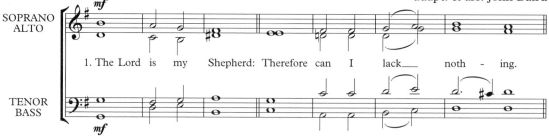

1. The Lord is my Shepherd: Therefore can I lack___ noth - ing.

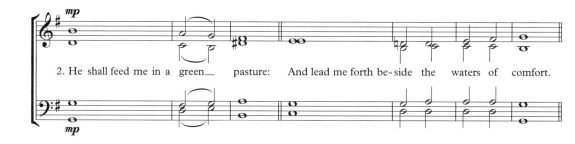

2. He shall feed me in a green___ pasture: And lead me forth be-side the waters of comfort.

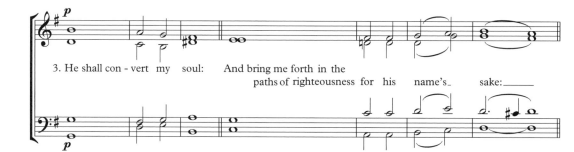

3. He shall con - vert my soul: And bring me forth in the
paths of righteousness for his name's___ sake:_____

4. Yea, though I walk through the
valley of the shadow of death, I will fear no evil: For thou art with me, thy rod and thy staff___ comfort me.

5. Thou shalt prepare a table
   before me, against them that trouble me: Thou has anointed my head with oil, and my cup shall be full._____

6. But thy loving kindness and
   mercy shall follow me, all the days of my life: And I will dwell in the house of the Lord for ever.

Glory be to the Father, and to the Son: And to the Ho - ly Ghost:_____

As it was in the beginning *
   is now and ev - er shall be: World without end. A - - men.

Psalm 42

Sicut cervus

Samuel Sebastian Wesley
(1810-1876)

SOPRANO
ALTO

1. Like as the hart de-sireth   the waterbrooks: So longeth my soul af-ter thee O God.

TENOR
BASS

2. My soul is athirst for God, *
   yea even for the   liv - ing God:

When shall I come
to appear, be-fore   the   presence of   God?

3. My tears have been
   my meat, day   and   night:

While they daily say
unto me, Where   is   now   thy   God?

4. Now when I think thereupon, *
   I pour out my heart   by my - self:

For I went with the multitude, *
and brought them   forth into the house of God.

53

5. In the voice of praise and thanksgiving: Among such as keep___ holy - day.

6. Why art thou so full of heaviness O my soul? And why art thou so dis - quieted with - in me?

7. Put thy trust in God: For I will yet give him thanks for the help of his countenance.

Glory be to the Father, and to the Son: And to the Ho - ly Ghost:

As it was in the beginning *
   is now and ev - er shall be: World without end.___ A - men.

Psalm 121

Levavi oculos

James Turle (1802-82)

1. I will lift up mine eyes unto the hills: From whence___ cometh my help.

2. My help cometh even from the Lord: Who hath made heav'n and earth.

3. He will not suffer thy foot to be moved: And he that keepeth thee will not sleep.

4. Behold, he that keep - eth Israel: Shall nei - ther slumber nor sleep.

5. The Lord himself is thy keeper: The Lord is thy defence up -on thy right___ hand;

6. So that the sun shall not burn thee by day: Neither the moon___ by___ night.

7. The Lord shall preserve thee from all___ evil: Yea it is even he that shall keep thy soul.

8. The Lord shall preserve thy going out and thy com - ing in: From this time forth for ev - er - more.

Glory be to the Father, and to the Son: And to the Ho - ly Ghost:

As it was in the beginning *
is now and ev - er shall be: World without end. A - - men.

Psalm 130

De profundis

James Turle (1802-82)
after Henry Purcell (1659-95)

1. Out of the deep have I called unto thee O Lord: Lord, hear my voice.

2. O let thine ears con - sid - er well: The voice of my com - plaint.

3. If thou, Lord, will be extreme to mark what is done a - miss: O Lord, who may a - bide it?

4. For there is mercy with thee: Therefore shalt thou be feared.

5. I look for the Lord, my soul doth wait for him: In his word is my trust.

Nunc dimittis

Luke 2: 29-32

John Goss (1800-80) after
Ludwig van Beethoven (1770-1827)

1. Lord now lettest thou thy servant de - part in peace: Ac - cor-ding to thy word.

2. For mine eyes have seen thy sal - vation. Which thou hast prepared before the face of all people.

3. To be a light to lighten the Gentiles: And to be the glory of thy peo - ple Israel.

Glory be to the Father, and to the Son: And to the Ho - ly Ghost:

As it was in the beginning *
is now and ev - er shall be: World without end. A - men.

for Harold and Marion, Joan and her family

Alleluia

Antiphon for Eastertide

Auroro lucis: Medieval
tr. T.A. Lacey (1853-1931)

Plainsong melody

The sad a - pos - tles mourn him, slain, Nor hope to— see their Lord— a - gain,

When, to their ver - y eyes— re - stored, They look— up - on— the— ri - sen Lord.

Antiphon for Ascensiontide

Mark 16: 19

Viri Galilei: Medieval
adapt. John Baird

Af - ter the Lord——— had spo - ken un - to them, He was re - ceiv - ed

up— in - to heav'n; And he sat— at the right hand— of God

Vivace leggero

John Baird

SOPRANO

Al - - le - lu - ia, al - le - lu -

ALTO

Al - - le - lu - ia,——— al - le -

TENOR

Al - le - lu - ia, al - le - lu -

BASS

Al - le - - lu - ia, al - le - lu -

Vivace leggero

* descant should be sung if possible.

Almighty and everlasting God

Collect for the Third
Sunday after Epiphany

Orlando Gibbons (1583-1625)

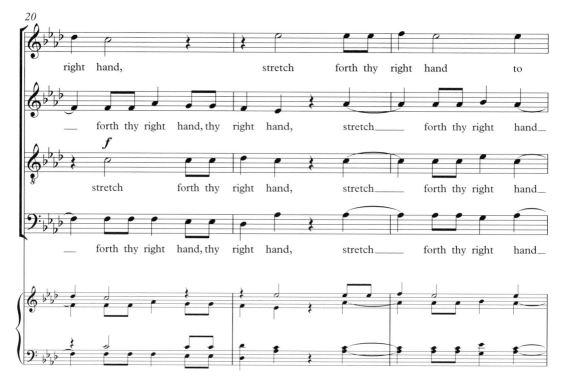

for Maeve and Annie

Ave Maria

Anon.

J.S. Bach (1685-1750)
& Charles Gounod (1818-93)
arr. John Baird

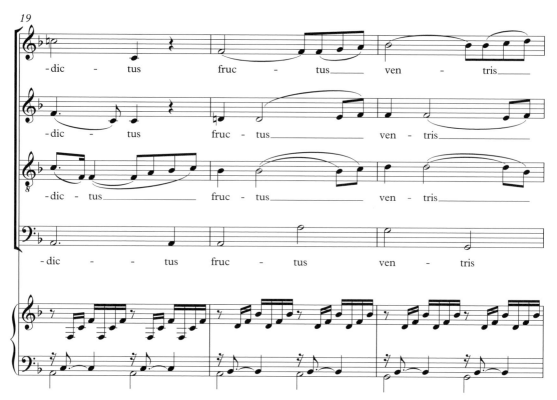

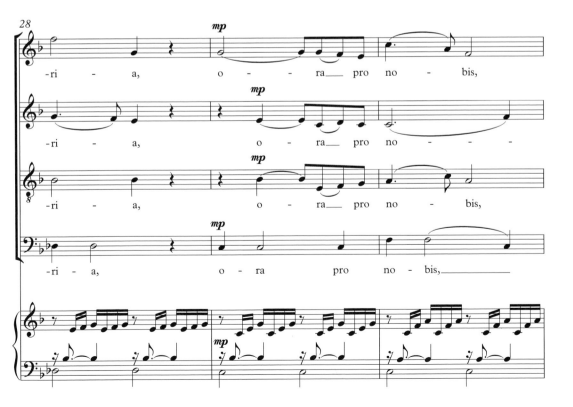

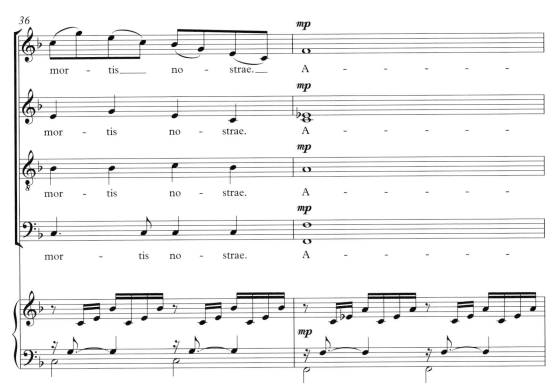

for Justin

Ave Maria

Anon.

Franz Schubert (1797-1828)
arr. John Baird

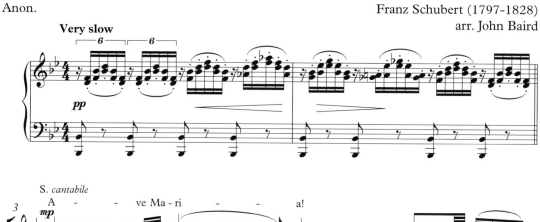

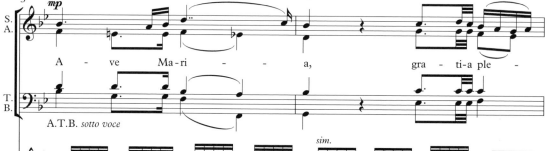

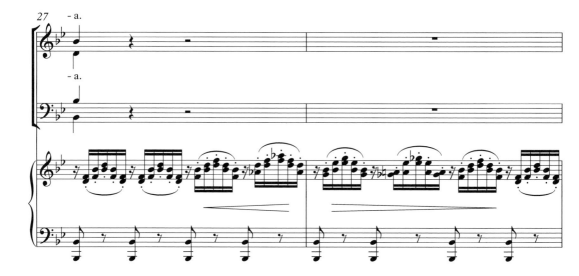

Ave verum corpus

14th-century hymn

William Byrd (1543-1623)

Ave verum corpus

14th-century hymn

Edward Elgar (1857–1934)

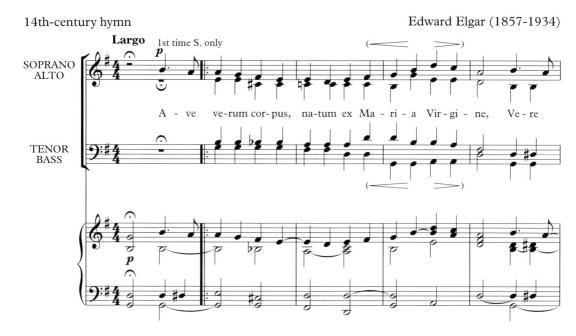

A - ve ve-rum cor-pus, na-tum ex Ma - ri - a Vir-gi - ne, Ve - re

pas-sum, im - mo - la - tum in cru - ce pro ho - mi - ne. A - ve - ne. Cu - ius

Ave verum corpus

14th-century hymn

Wolfgang Amadeus Mozart
(1756–91)

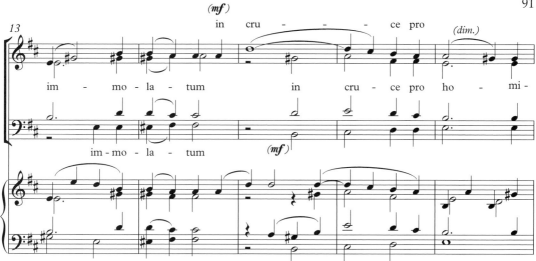

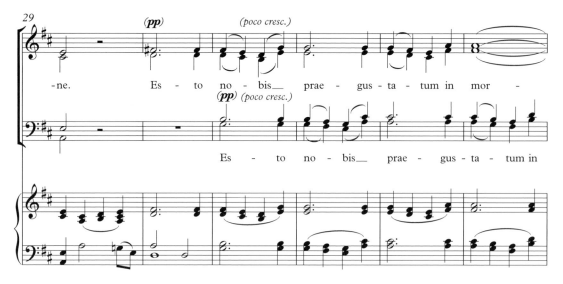

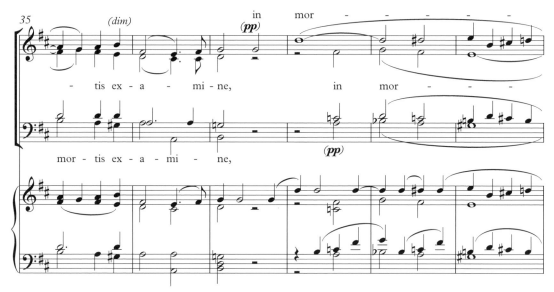

for Lucy, Rick, Jemima and Suzanna

Canon

an elaboration for SATB

Psalm 84
English version: John Baird

Johann Pachelbel (1653-1706)
abridged & arr. John Baird

allargando poco

revised and abridged January 2014

Creation's Hymn

Die Ehre Gottes aus der Natur

Words adapt. John Baird
from various sources

Ludwig van Beethoven (1770-1827)
arr. John Baird

The heav'ns are tell - ing the glo - ry of God.___ The

earth calls out his wond - 'rous___ name. The light, the dark - ness, the

The heav'ns are tell - ing the glo - ry of God.___ The

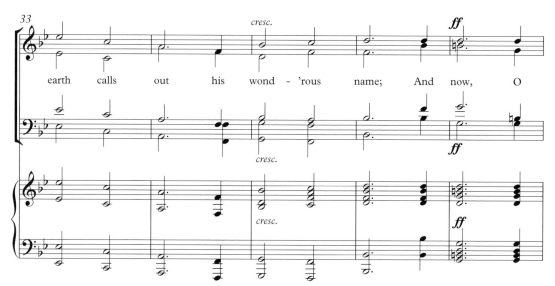

earth calls out his wond - 'rous name; And now, O

man, God's pow'r pro - claim!

If ye love me

John 14: 15-17

Thomas Tallis (1505-85)

for Jack

Gaudete

Piae Cantiones (1582)
adapt. John Baird

Gau – de – te, gau – de – te Christ – us est na – tus

ex Ma – ri – a Vir – gi – ne, gau – de – te!

Refrain 1

Gau – de – te, gau – de – te Christ – us est na – tus

ex Ma – ri – a Vir – gi – ne, gau – de – te!

(SOLO or UNIS.)

1. Tem – pus ad – est gra – ti – ae hoc quod op – ta – ba – mus,

Car – mi – na lae – ti – ti – ae de – vo – te red – da – mus.

To refrain

* Optional drone for singers or instruments.

2. De - us ho - mo fac - tus est na - tu - ra mi - ran - te,

To refrain

Mun - dus re - no - va - tus est a Christ - o reg - nan - te.

3. Ez - e - chi - e - lis por - ta clau - sa per - tran - si - tur,

To refrain

Un - de lux est or - ta sa - lus in - ven - i - tur.

4. Er - go nos - tra con - ti - o psal - lat iam in lus - tro,

To refrain

Be - ne - di - cat Do - mi - no; sa - lus Re - gi nos - tro.

ff Refrain 2

S. A.

Gau - de - te, gau - de - te Christ - us est na - tus

T. B.

ff

1. 2. *dim.* **Fine**

ex Ma - ri - a Vir - gi - ne, gau - de - te! te!

dim.

* Verses 2 & 3 may sung to same tune as verse 1.
If desired, the music of verses 2 & 3 can be sung together.
The refrains can be mixed and matched as desired, though the small notes in Refrain 2 should only be sung the final time.

Glory to God

from Messiah

Luke 2: 14

George Frideric Handel
(1685-1759)

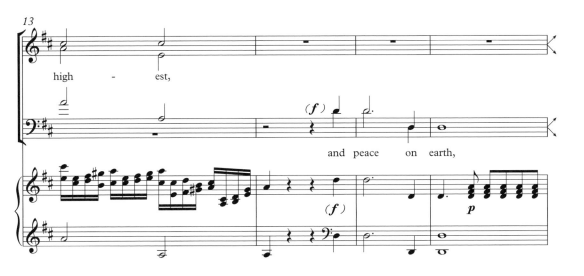

good - will, good - will to - ward men, good - will to -

good - will, good - will to-ward men, good - will

good - will, good - will to-ward men, good - will

good - will, good - will to - ward men, good - will

- ward men.

to - ward men.

to - ward men.

to - ward men.

Jesu, joy of man's desiring

from Cantata No. 147

Robert Bridges (1844-1930)

J.S. Bach (1685-1750)

Ho - ly wis - dom, love___ most___ bright.

souls as - pir - ing,

Drawn by thee,__ our souls as - pir - ing,

souls__ as - pir - ing,

Soar__ to un - cre - a - ted__ light.

un - cre - a - ted light.

love_____ of joys_____ un - - known.

In memoriam John Marrs Baird

Largo
(from *Xerxes*)

De profundis

Charles Wesley (1707-1788)
(adapted) **(Larghetto)**

George Frideric Handel (1685-1759)
arr. John Baird

Lord, leave me not a - lone, but hear my cry!

Lord, hear my prayer!

God be in my head

Sarum Primer, 1538

Henry Walford Davies (1869-1941)

* cue-sized notes should be sung if forces allow.

Laudate Dominum

from Solemn Vespers KV 339

Psalm 117

Wolfgang Amadeus Mozart
(1756-91)

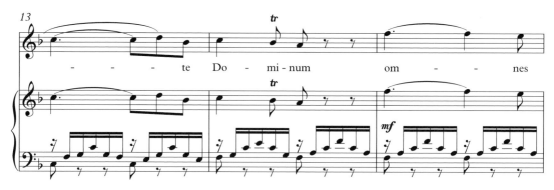

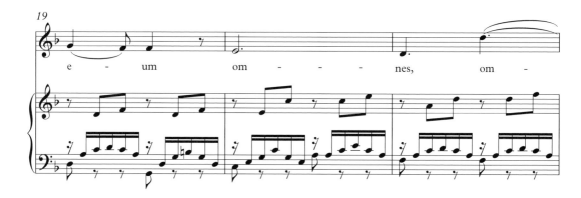

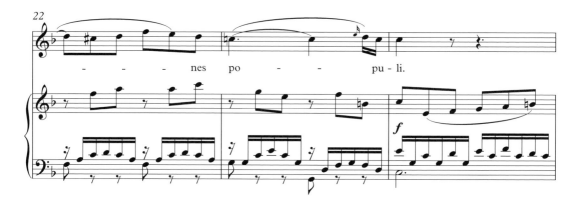

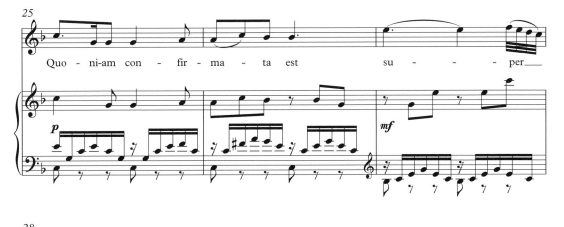

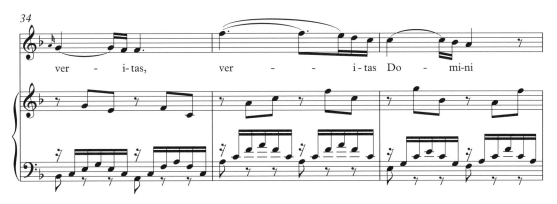

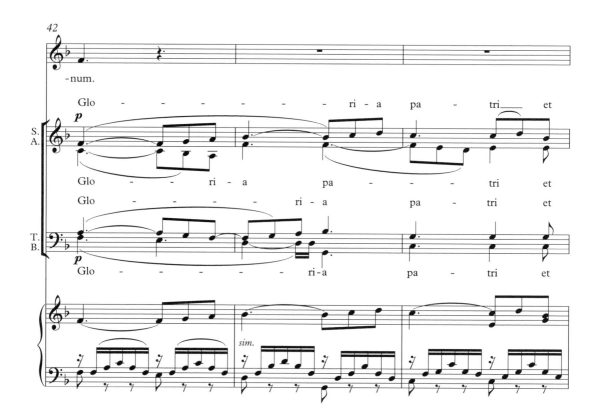

fi - li - o et spi - ri - tu - i sanc - to,

si - - - cut e - - -

- rat in prin - ci - - pi - o

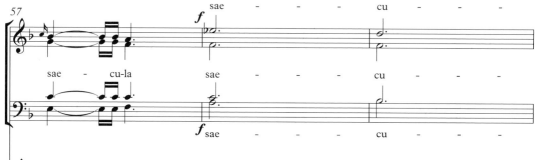

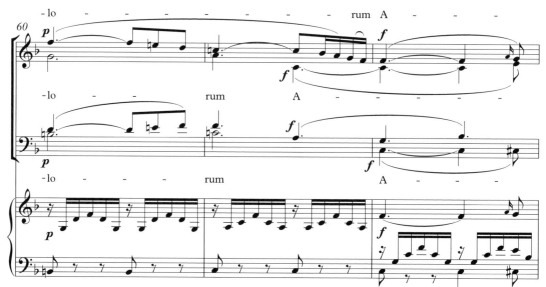

Lead me, Lord

Psalm 5: 8 & 4: 8

Samuel Sebastian Wesley
(1810-76)

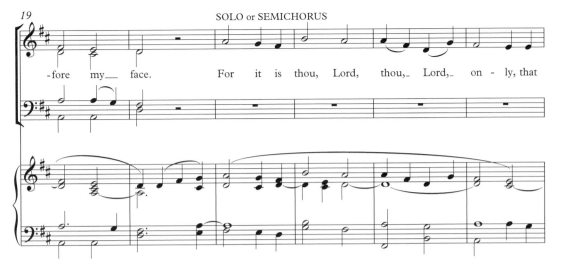

Locus iste

Gradual for a
Dedication Mass

Anton Bruckner (1824-96)

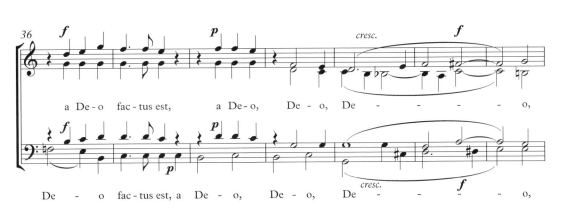

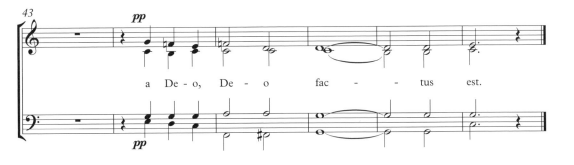

Now thank we all our God

Martin Rinkart (1586-1649)
tr. Catherine Winkworth (1827-78)

Johann Crüger (1598-1662)
harm. J.S. Bach (1685-1750) &
Johann Pachelbel (1653-1706)

shall now be giv-en; Let us now sing with

joy and give praise and thanks to God; praise and thanks to God.

D.C.

He who looks o-ver us, the one e-ter-nal God.

O for the wings of a dove

from Hear my prayer

Psalm 55. English version by
William Bartholomew (1793-1867)

Felix Mendelssohn (1809-47)

-main_ there for ev - er at rest,_____ in the wil - der-ness build me, build me a nest;_

and re - main there for ev - er at rest, in__ the wil-der-ness build me a nest;_

and re - main there for ev - er at rest, and_____ re - main_ there for

ev - er at rest, and_____ re - main_ there for ev - - - er at

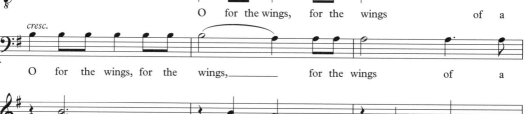

* cue-sized notes
for rehearsal only

* cue-sized notes
  for rehearsal only

for the friends in Medici Choir

O God, thou art my God

from Psalm 63

Henry Purcell (1659-95)
abridged & adapt. John Baird

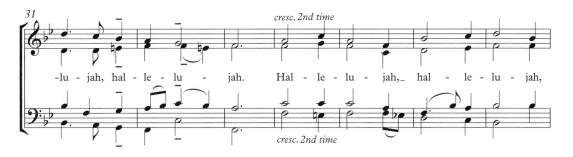

for James and Rosie

O Holy night!

Cantique de Noël

Placide Cappeau (1808-77)
English version: J.S. Dwight (1813-93)

Adolphe Adam (1803-56)
arr. John Baird

Andante maestoso

SOLO

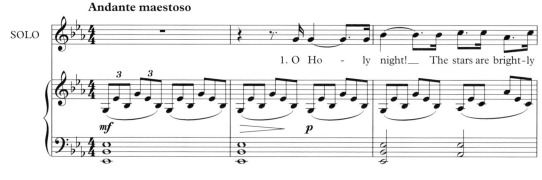

1. O Ho - ly night!__ The stars are bright-ly

shin - ing, It is the night of the dear Sa-viour's birth.

Long lay the world__ in sin and er - ror pin - ing Till he ap-
So led by light of a star sweet-ly gleam - ing Here came the

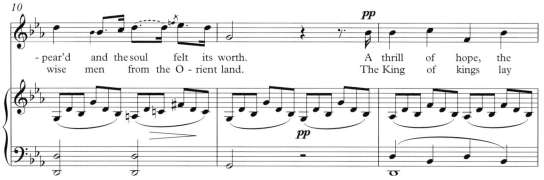

- pear'd and the soul felt its worth. A thrill of hope, the
wise men from the O - rient land. The King of kings lay

wea - ry world re - joi - ces, For yon - der breaks a new and glo - rious morn.
thus in low - ly man - ger, In all our tri - als born to be our friend,

Fall on your knees! Oh hear the an - gel
He knows our need, He guard - eth us from

Fall on your knees! Oh
He knows our need, He

Fall on your knees! Oh,
He knows our need, He

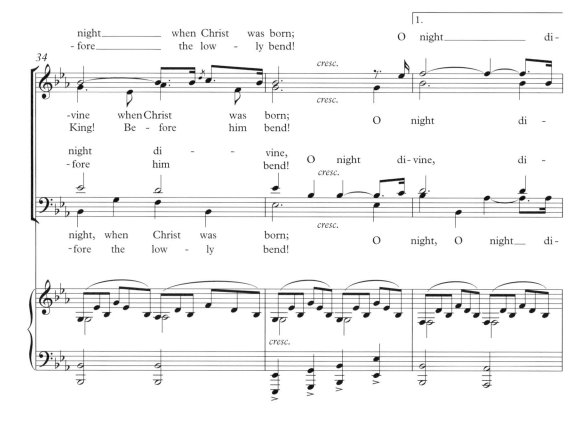

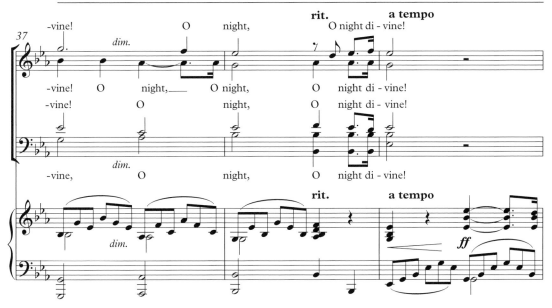

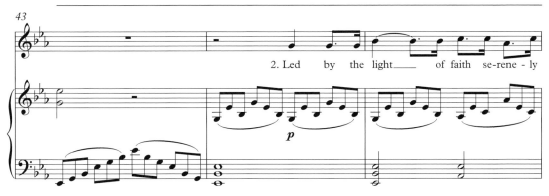

158

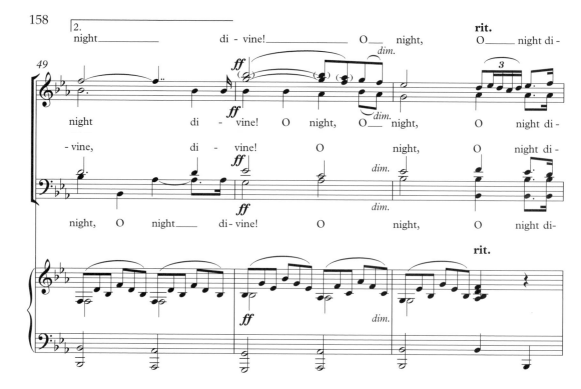

for Felicity and Lesley

Panis angelicus

Thomas Aquinas (1225-74)

César Franck (1822-90)
adapt. John Baird

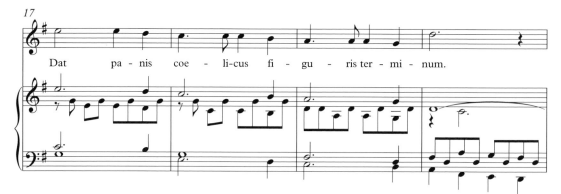

Dat pa - nis coe - li-cus fi - gu - ris ter - mi - num.

O res mi - ra - bi - lis! man - du - cat Do-mi-num,

Pau - per, pau - per, ser - vus et hu - mi - lis,

Pau - per, pau - per, ser - vus et hu - mi - lis.

for Juliet and Freya

Sheep may safely graze

Words adapt. John Baird
from various sources

J.S. Bach (1685-1750)
adapt. and arr. by John Baird

well.

well.

When the world is ruled with__ wis - dom,__

Fine

we shall then know__ the ma - ny__ bles - sings which both peace and__

the ma - ny bles-sings which__ both__ peace and

* Bach's original marking is D.C.

for Mairi and Esmé

Thou visitest the earth

from Psalm 65

Maurice Greene (1696-1755)
arr. John Baird

good - ness, thou crown - est the___ year, the year with thy good - ness.

good - ness, thou___ crown - est the year with thy good - ness.

good - ness, thou crown - est the year with thy good - ness. Thou

good - ness, thou crown - est the year with thy good - ness.

Thou vi - sit - est the earth, and bless-est it, and bless-est it. Thou

Thou vi - sit - est the___ earth___ and bless-est it.

vi - sit - est the Earth, thou vi - sit - est the earth, and bless-est it.

Thou vi - sit - est the earth, and bless-est it. Thou

* optional ornamentation

Thou knowest, Lord, the secrets of our hearts

from *Music for the Funeral of Queen Mary*

Book of Common Prayer

Henry Purcell (1659-95)

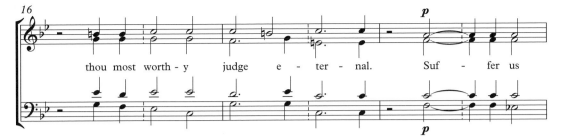

1 2 3 4 5 6 7 8 9